GHOST MONEY

GHOST
MONEY

Lynda Hull

The University of Massachusetts Press
Amherst   1986

Library of Congress Cataloging-in-Publication Data
Hull, Lynda, 1954–
  Ghost money.
  I. Title.
PS3558.U323G5   1986   811'.54   86–14216
ISBN 0–87023–545–1 (alk. paper)
ISBN 0–87023–546–X (pbk.: alk. paper)

Ghost Money has been published with the support of the Literature Program of
the National Endowment for the Arts, a federal agency to which acknowledg-
ment is gratefully made.

Acknowledgment is made to the following publications where some of these
poems appeared, sometimes in earlier versions:

Antioch Review 44, no. 2 (Spring 1986), "Maquillage," "The Bookkeeper,"
and "Little Elegies," copyright © 1986 by The Antioch Review, Inc.; Crazy-
horse, "Accretion," "Arias, 1971," and "1933"; Indiana Review, "Prepar-
ing the Estate Sale" and "Remington"; Missouri Review, "Night Waitress";
The New Yorker, April 1, 1985, "Jackson Hotel"; North American Review,
Fall 1984, "Autumn Mist"; Poetry, "Chinese New Year" and "Insect Life of
Florida"; Poetry Northwest, "The Fitting"; Sonora Review, "Hollywood
Jazz"; Telescope 3, no. 3, "Invisible Gestures"; and Tendril, "Tide of
Voices."

"The Charmed Hour" and "Housekeeping Cottages" were included in The
Grolier Poetry Prize Annual (1984).

I would like to thank David Jauss, Elizabeth Spires, Denis Johnson, Richard
Lyons, and all of my teachers in life whose care helped make this book possible.

"Night Waitress" is for Maureen McCoy, "Remington" is for Richard and
Maura, and "Diamonds" is for Yusef.

for David, for Jeanne, and for my family

"White, through white cities passed on to
assume that world which comes to each of us
alone."
  Hart Crane

"And all things are forgiven . . . it would be
strange not to forgive."
  Chekhov

Contents

Three

GHOST MONEY

Spell for the Manufacture & Use of a
Magic Carpet

When the last commuter trains etch
black signatures of departure over tracks
and subways glide untroubled through quiet tunnels,
find an obscure girl. Let her weave a carpet
of white & new wool, the best wool

of the Garment District. Obtain a wand
from the Armenian in the hour of the sun
when the moon is full & in Capricorn. Go to a park
or a rooftop where you'll suffer no disturbance.
Spread your carpet facing East & West,

& having drawn a circle to enclose it,
hold your wand in the air. Name backward
the chain of names from each current of the past into
whatever crests foamless toward the future.
Invoke the faces abandoned in cloakrooms

of childhood, summoning each discarded
voice. Thank each panicked corridor & lucid
clinic doorway, blessing the hands that ministered
to you for they have carried you to this
wild incompletion. Remember them,

shed them in the East & North,
to the South & West, raising in turn each
of the carpet's corners. Go home. Fold your carpet
until you need it. Order your house
& remove each dooryard stone.

Wait for a night of full or new moon
when open windows free the sleepers' heated breath.
On a roof where you'll risk no harm, write with a feather,
on a strip of azure parchment, those characters
found on page three hundred and seven

in the Dictionary of Angels. Hold
the wand in your left hand, the parchment
in your right, recite the arcana of angels for each
precinct. Thank whatever god you understand,
whatever buoys you past

each harbored absence. Ask then
to discover the secret thing you seek,
gazing out always over the diners & arcades
to the cities of New Jersey rising
white, small beyond the Palisades.

ONE

Tide of Voices

At the hour the streetlights come on, buildings
turn abstract. The Hudson, for a moment, formal.
We drink bourbon on the terrace and you speak
in the evening voice, weighted deep in the throat.

They plan to harvest oysters, you tell me,
from the harbor by Jersey City, how the waters
will be clean again in twenty years. I imagine nets
burdened with rough shells, the meat dun and sexual.

Below, the river and the high rock
where boys each year jump from bravado
or desperation. The day flares, turns into itself.
And innocently, sideways, the way we always fall

into grace or knowledge, we watched the police
drag the river for a suicide, the third this year.
The terrible hook, the boy's frail whiteness.
His face was blank and new as your face

in the morning before the day has worked
its pattern of lines and tensions. A hook
like an iron question and this coming
out of the waters, a flawed pearl—

a memory that wasn't ours to claim.
Perhaps, in a bedroom by lamplight,
a woman waits for this boy. She may riffle drawers
gathering photographs, string, keys to abandoned rooms.

Even now she may be leaving,
closing the door for some silence. I need

to move next to you. Water sluiced
from the boy's hair. I need to watch you

light your cigarette, the flickering
of your face in matchlight, as if underwater,
drifting away. I take your cigarette
and drag from it, touch your hand.

Remember that winter of your long fever,
the winter we understood how fragile
any being together was. The wall sweated
behind the headboard and you said you felt

the rim where dreams crouch
and every room of the past. It must begin in luxury—
do you think—a break and fall into the glamour
attending each kind of surrender. Water must flood

the mind, as in certain diseases, the walls
between the cells of memory dissolve, blur
into a single stream of voices and faces.
I don't know any more about this river or if

it can be cleaned of its tender and broken histories—
a tide of voices. And this is how the dead
rise to us, transformed: wet and singing,
the tide of voices pearling in our hands.

Insect Life of Florida

In those days I thought their endless thrum
    was the great wheel that turned the days, the nights.
        In the throats of hibiscus and oleander

I'd see them clustered yellow, blue, their shells
    enamelled hard as the sky before rain.
        All that summer, my second, from city

to city my young father drove the black coupe
    through humid mornings I'd wake to like fever
        parcelled between luggage and sample goods.

Afternoons, showers drummed the roof,
    my parents silent for hours. Even then I knew
        something of love was cruel, was distant.

Mother leaned over the seat to me, the orchid
    Father'd pinned in her hair shrivelled
        to a purple fist. A necklace of shells

coiled her throat, moving a little as she
    murmured of alligators that float the rivers
        able to swallow a child whole, of mosquitoes

whose bite would make you sleep a thousand years.
    And always the trance of blacktop shimmering
        through swamps with names like incantations—

Okeefenokee, where Father held my hand
    and pointed to an egret's flight unfolding
        white above swamp reeds that sang with insects

until I was lost, until I was part
    of the singing, their thousand wings gauze
        on my body, tattooing my skin.

Father rocked me later by the water,
    on the motel balcony, singing calypso
        above the Jamaican radio. The lyrics

a net over the sea, its lesson
    of desire and repetition. Lizards flashed
        over his shoes, over the rail

where the citronella burned, merging our
    shadows—Father's face floating over mine
        in the black changing sound

of night, the enormous Florida night,
    metallic with cicadas, musical
        and dangerous as the human heart.

The Fitting

The room smelled of steam
the day my tall sad mother
brought me to watch
the fitting. Heat knocked
old pipes below the window
where I sat, cheek cradled
on the pane, elbow
pushed among violets
and cactus crowding the sill.
Murmuring of patterns,
the women unfolded damask
my father had brought
from Turkey, almost
too heavy for the afternoon.
The seamstress frightened me,
her hands discovering
my mother's shape
as she hummed
through the pins in her mouth.
I watched until
my head ached
and felt thin as glass.
In the sky
wind milled clouds, promised
no animals or countries.
Only seamless gray.
My tongue was difficult,
sullen as the buildings
repeating a red-brick phrase

down the street.
I pricked my finger
on the cactus—said nothing,
hearing the silence
in the room. Then, I saw
my mother step toward me
changing the air.
In the dimness,
I touched my hair,
the same soft hair
that aureoled her face.
A bright drop welled
on my finger, and everywhere,
the scent of violets, steam.

1933

Whole countries hover, oblivious on the edge
of history and in Cleveland the lake
already is dying. None of this matters
to my mother at seven, awakened from sleep

to follow her father through darkened rooms
downstairs to the restaurant emptied
of customers, chairs stacked and steam glazing
the window, through the kitchen bright with pans,

ropes of kielbasa, the tubs of creamy lard
that resemble, she thinks, ice cream.
At the tavern table her father's friends
talk rapidly to a man in a long gray coat,

in staccato French, Polish, harsh German.
Her mother stops her, holds her shoulders, and whispers
This is a famous man. Remember his face.
Trotsky—a name like one of her mother's

fond, strange nouns. He looks like the man
who makes her laugh at Saturday matinées,
only tired. So tired. Her father pours the man
another drink of clear, bootleg gin, then turns

smiling to her. She has her own glass.
Peppermint schnapps that burns and makes her light,
cloudy so grown-ups forget her when she curls
on a bench and drifts then wakes and drifts again.

At the bar, her mother frowns, braids shining
round her head bent to the books, the columns

of figures in her bold hand and the smoke, voices
of men, a wash of syllables she sleeps upon

until her father wakes her to the empty room.
The men are gone. A draft of chill air lingers
in her father's hair, his rough shirt,
and together they walk the block to morning Mass.

Still dark and stars falter, then wink sharp
as shattered mirrors. Foghorns moan
and the church is cold. A few women in babushkas
kneel in the pews. Still dizzy, she follows

the priest's litanies for those who wait within
life's pale, for those departed, the shades humming
in the air, clustered thick as lake fog in the nave.
The priest elevates the wafer, a pale day moon

the spirit of God leafs through, then it's
a human face—her father's, the tired man's
and she is lost and turning through fragrant air.
Her fingers entwined make a steeple, but

all she sees is falling: the church collapsing
in shards, the great bell tolling, tolling.
1933 outside and some unwound mainspring has set
the world careening. The Jazz Age

ended years ago. Lean olive-skinned men
sport carnations and revolvers, and in the country
of her father, bankers in threadbare morning coats
wheel cartloads of currency to the bakeries

for a single loaf. The men who wait each night
outside the kitchen door have a look she's seen
in her father's eyes, although it's two years
until he turns his gentle hand against himself.

But now he touches her face. Her father stands
so straight, as if wearing a uniform he's proud of.
She watches him shape the sign of the cross.
She crosses forehead, lips, and breast, and believes,

for a moment, her father could cradle the world
in his palm. When they leave the church and its flickering
votive candles for market, it is dawn. The milkman's
wagon horse waits, patient at the curb, his breath

rosettes of steam rising to the sky that spills
like a pail of blue milk across morning. She prays
that God take care of the man in the gray coat,
that her father will live forever.

The Bookkeeper

I know the way evening shawls the mirror,
the bureau where years ago
my brother kept a lacquered box
beside the brush with its cinnabar handle.
Inside were coins, small rounds flashing
the profiles of queens and archdukes, tyrants
only history's long memory preserves.
He said we were difficult music, an endless

glissando of moods. He leaned over my shoulder
and made the shapes of notes, cupping my hands,
the keys. Tonight, the numbers are precise,
the ledger closed on the desk. I cover
the typewriter and walk home. For a moment
twilight kindles iridescent
the feathers of roosters
the Chinese grocer stacks in bamboo cages,

the strange privacy of my face through bars,
and a bird's flurry disturbing,
becoming the composition.
The first magnolias in the park
unfurl, their scent
almost an injury. Against my palm
the cane's handle curves smooth. My foot
lists in its heavy shoe.

Half a lifetime since my brother
sat with me—the operations and long shuttered
evenings with the iced drinks of summer.
He played Strauss when the gauze was removed.

He lifted me and waltzed across
the parquet, my face tucked against his neck,
the scent of bay rum. The phonograph played
into circles of static, circles of silence.

Last night I burned unanswered the letters
written on the stationery of foreign hotels.
The last from Spain, its single olive leaf
silver and bitter if held to the lips.
I imagine him ending in a port city
handling the morning papers
with gloved hands so acid won't taint
his fingers, still formal and elegant.

What could I have written? That
I don't remember his face? That I must
sit in the park with those who sit
and hear leaves blade the air, sharp,
then faltering like a flute breaking
into raggedness? That above us
the statue of a general towers? In the radiance
of streetlamps his hand extends,

as if blessing, as if conducting the orchestra
of musicians accident has assembled below him.

Night Waitress

Reflected in the plate glass, the pies
look like clouds drifting off my shoulder.
I'm telling myself my face has character,
not beauty. It's my mother's Slavic face.
She washed the floor on hands and knees
below the Black Madonna, praying
to her god of sorrows and visions
who's not here tonight when I lay out the plates,
small planets, the cups and moons of saucers.
At this hour the men all look
as if they'd never had mothers.
They do not see me. I bring the cups.
I bring the silver. There's the man
who leans over the jukebox nightly
pressing the combinations
of numbers. I would not stop him
if he touched me, but it's only songs
of risky love he leans into. The cook sings
with the jukebox, a moan and sizzle
into the grill. On his forehead
a tattooed cross furrows,
diminished when he frowns. He sings words
dragged up from the bottom of his lungs.
I want a song that rolls
through the night like a big Cadillac
past factories to the refineries
squatting on the bay, round and shiny
as the coffee urn warming my palm.
Sometimes when coffee cruises my mind

visiting the most remote way stations,
I think of my room as a calm arrival
each book and lamp in its place. The calendar
on my wall predicts no disaster
only another white square waiting
to be filled like the desire that fills
jail cells, the old arrest
that makes me stare out the window or want
to try every bar down the street.
When I walk out of here in the morning
my mouth is bitter with sleeplessness.
Men surge to the factories and I'm too tired
to look. Fingers grip lunch box handles,
belt buckles gleam, wind riffles my uniform
and it's not romantic when the sun unlids
the end of the avenue. I'm fading
in the morning's insinuations
collecting in the crevices of buildings,
in wrinkles, in every fault
of this frail machinery.

Maquillage

After nestling champagne splits in ice
I'd line the bottles behind the bar. Tapped,
they made a chilly music, *an arsenal
of bells* you called it. When I circled my arms
around myself I could count ribs
under my cotton shift. Rochelle sat at the stage's
edge warming her satin costume. She
couldn't bear the cold cloth. On the way
to your rooms I'd adjust blue lights for her.

René, that year you were the only father
I'd admit. Before opening each evening
we'd sip wine coolers on the balcony,
watch the day burn out over the square
and fountain with its cluster of stone cherubs.

With a straight razor you'd shave your face,
clean, then smooth indigo on your lids
and draw the lines of your mouth. Nights
you shook too much I'd do your face,
the wig, make you talk. It became a way
of managing the days, evening's slow descent
until the city turned in its fever
and music rose through the floor.

I'd serve while Rochelle balanced
on a sequined ball, stepping down
to the blown sound of blues. She'd gyrate
till she'd lost it all and you'd glide, joking
among tables, benevolent in a rayon kimono.

All night the river of men swerved
under their solitary stars, and we'd go on

minor players waking startled to the care
or harm of unlikely hands, surprised
to hit the lights and find the place
so shabby: numbers on the wall, the butts
and broken glass. Quiet after closing,
I'd lean by the door and smoke, hear
the fountain erode cherub faces.

You're nowhere I know anymore René.
The future we predicted is the past
and different. You're the empty room
morning pours into through a torn shade,
that place you said most nearly spells peace
in the heart, narrow glasses on the ledge
reflecting the horizon.

Tonight, children's quarreling rises
from the yard. For a moment, through shutters
the city relights itself until it's time
for music to shiver the floorboards,
the hour of plumage . . .

But that was long ago. I was only seventeen.

Jackson Hotel

Sometimes after hours of wine I can almost see
   the night gliding in low off the harbor
      down the long avenues of shop windows

past mannequins, perfect in their gestures.
   I leave water steaming on the gas ring
      and sometimes I can slip from my body,

almost find the single word to prevent evenings
   that absolve nothing, a winter lived alone
      and cold. Rooms where you somehow marry

the losses of strangers that tremble
   on the walls like the hands
      of the dancer next door, luminous

with Methedrine, she taps walls for hours
   murmuring about the silver she swears
      lines the building, the hallways

where each night drunks stammer their
   usual rosary until they come to rest
      beneath the tarnished numbers, the bulbs

that star each ceiling.
   I must tell you I am afraid to sit here
      losing myself to the hour's slow erasure

until I know myself only by this cold weight,
   this hand on my lap, palm up.
      I want to still the dancer's hands

in mine, to talk about forgiveness
and what we leave behind—faces
and cities, the small emergencies

of nights. I say nothing, but
leaning on the sill, I watch her leave
at that moment

when the first taxis start rolling
to the lights of Chinatown, powered
by sad and human desire. I watch her fade

down the street until she's a smudge,
violet in the circle of my breath. A figure
so small I could cup her in my hands.

TWO

Little Elegies

I don't know if Bonnard
would have painted the scene from my window.
Five-twenty in the morning
and the black walnut with its branch of yellow leaves
curves over the rooftops of Poole Foundry
wet from rain. In the parking lot below
a nameless agitator was shot two hours ago,
stalled for a moment beneath the blue lights
of emergency, the squad cars and pulsing sirens.

Bonnard painted wholly from memory the casual gestures
of the streets, the kitchen garden at Le Cannet
seen from the window and, with what must have been
great love, his wife Marthe. I have two prints of her
on my wall, pinned together in the way the painter worked,
two or three canvases at once.

Here he's painted a little elegy—the Midi's
transient light yellow in this print, a standing nude.
The leg of the vanity repeats in the mirror reflecting
an armoire as if the room should divide into
a series of rooms, but it's only an equation
for the atmosphere touching Marthe's back,
a lock of hair escaping her chignon. Her hand,
almost shyly, is cupped before her.

Twenty years later, Marthe is in the bath
dissolving in the wash of light on tiles
ultramarine to viridian. I can complete
what the painter leaves out: his wife crushing
lavender into water, the flowering almonds

swaying in the wind outside the house.
His way of resolving the violence of time
on his wife's body was a gentle arrest
in a churning memory of light.

He sang when he painted, eyes squinted
behind steel-framed glasses, and somehow
sitting here this fragile hour as day ignites,
it helps to watch the shadows on Marthe's ankle,
the severe yellow arch of her foot
in its violet shoe. I can almost complete

the man's face. It was mottled. On the wet pavement
rain made little shining rivers beneath his white hand,
the fingers curved almost shyly to his palm.
The sky grows lavender, the bricks sienna.
These colors, Bonnard said, *bewilder me.*

Contagion

The air swamps, static, overheated,
the kind of weather that founders a city
before a plague occurs. A fever of starlings
weights the oak's thick branches, their
nattering cries—*sex, sex*. The leaves sear
hectic as the consumptive heroine's cheeks
in the pages of the 19th-century novel
you read before the open window. She dies
so piteously; her young aristocrat bears
orchids to the antiseptic charity ward
too late to say it mattered. She coughs.
You close the book. The air stains now
with smoke, the farmers clearing stubble
from fields in this dim province of burning.

Autumn, Mist

1

This morning I took the wine from the sill
glazed perfectly in ice. It smoked down my throat,
mist across autumn fields I left in Maine
thirty years ago. I asked the mirror
if this is what it means: another room
known by heart, the Charles below
accepting everything. The city I saw on postcards
was a lie. Those shots from above, all light.

Father, my face is yours,
the way I last saw you flickering
in the doorway, tired as your eighty acres
of salt marsh and scrub pine.
Meaningless to say you were right;
the night my feet failed on the stage
of a Park Square bar, I knew it.
The men didn't look up from their drinks.

This morning tracing wrinkles from
nose to chin, I imagined them folding forever
into darkness.
Fields, dance floors—same thing—places where
soil or rhythm breaks down, where we turn
to meet ourselves.

2

It was such a simple act,
the most precise.

The fingers on the razor
might have belonged to someone else.
Over the bed, the crack in the ceiling
like the border of a country
I could never quite recall. Water rushes
in pipes, the drain needs fixing.
In the dark, it doesn't matter.
My dancing shoes, worn down at the heels
lean against each other in the closet.

Jacques will creep
up the stairs, shoes in hand, tired
from waiting tables. He steps so lightly
as if his late return is a matter of concern.
He should always be serving, always be leaning
over candles, eyes mauved in strained circles.

He'll bring rolls in white paper
as always. Tomorrow, he'll unpin the print
from the wall, Picasso—a woman ironing,
everything falling in blue gravity,
so tired, as if she desires only to sink
from the weight of her body.

3

And, perhaps, the body
really is a gift, this small beating
in my ribs a reasoned rhythm. Once, a woman
at the museum reminded me of a harp. Her supple spine
defined a frame. She was so tense, I could see wires
as if at any moment she would become music
or break. The way moonlight broke itself

in our window when as children
we sisters cut each other's hair.
Mary and I found a moth trapped in butter—
wings
a purple diagram of stopped motion.

At Thirty

Whole years I knew only nights: automats
& damp streets, the Lower East Side steep

with narrow rooms where sleepers turn beneath
alien skies. I ran when doorways spoke

rife with smoke & zippers. But it was only the heart's
racketing flywheel stuttering *I want, I want*

until exhaustion, until I was a guest in the yoke
of my body by the last margin of land where the river

mingles with the sea & far off daylight whitens,
a rending & yielding I must kneel before, as

barges loose glittering mineral freight
& behind me façades gleam with pigeons

folding iridescent wings. Their voices echo
in my voice naming what is lost, what remains.

Diamonds

Only once had I seen the diamonds worn:
at the funeral of the scarlet parrot, my sister
draped herself in velvet, musty from the attic
trunk, then chanted over the shoebox we buried
with a watch and three Russian coins. On her hands
the rings sparkled a trance over geraniums
banked on the grave. I know I looked foolish,
a boy in black tights kneeling to smooth the earth.
I believed the soul was fire, and waited
that night for the bird to soar in flames
over the sleeping house, beyond Grandmother's
room thick with her odors of menthol and garlic.
We had only each other, Manya and I
and Grandmother, her long dying,
with that ivory backscratcher shaped like a claw
on her table. In her illness, she wished herself
back sometimes to the flat on Railroad Street,
or sealed again in the casket, smuggled
from her village to the sea, those rings pinned
in her blouse. There was no ease in this remembering.
She'd startle and cry out in the old language.
I carried the soup, the glass syringe, and I
wished her dead when I stood by the window, silent.
When she called *Petrushka, Petrushka,* I hid in drapes
that closed around me, many whispering hands.
Manya rubbed her legs with black salve, and when
Grandmother died, I did not watch for a wreath
of fire. We found rubles and war bonds
sewn in the mattress, and months after we discovered

useless currency stitched in dresses, folded
in books she could not read.

For fifteen years her room has been empty—the house
Manya's now. She does not like me to come there.
Still, it had been easy to slip the diamonds
from the trunk, to walk all night the streets
of narrow houses with my coat drawn close against
the first chills, the cramping muscles. Trees
rustle in my ears, pages from some vast police
report, loosing leaves over the avenues
and freight yards lit with ashcan fires.
Sometimes I long to be smoke, rising up, away
from the body's shrill needs, those acts and hours
gone wrong. After I touched her, I'd wash my hands
over and over. Last week I remembered this
by the window of my room. There was a moon like
an oily bubble in the sky and my hands on the sill
were those of a foreigner, each vein a river,
scarred. And who, this morning
among these faces filing to work, these clerks
and secretaries, would crave this embrace?
Yet aren't they all speechlessly in love
with bad news, some private disgrace sheltered
in a doorway among those spread out before me?

At the street of gin mills and penny-ante
arcades, I pause and smooth my sleeves.
The pawn sign is tarnished, the taste of myself
as I stand before the broker. On the wall
a photo of Sonny Liston shadowboxes a postcard—
Pope John gazing, serenely, above the broker's
lacquered pompadour. He watches me unravel
the handkerchief, then squinting through

his jeweler's glass, he slides the rings across
his velvet tray. Wings burn behind my eyes
when he calls the diamonds poor, as I nod
to a price too low. *All she'd wanted
were her saints, a little morphine.* The shop fan
inflicts its breeze over my face, and seized
by the trembling, I turn toward the street
where shadows pool like black waters, toward
the traffic's effortless passage. I'd risen
once from the waters of sleep
to my grandmother's face framed by the smoke
of her hair. In the nightlight, she stood
over me, as now, like an angel of reckoning
swayed by a powerful and secret weeping.

A System

All week, floods throughout the South.
Beneath a beer sign's floating rings
I wait for the rain to clear in this bar
where the patrons are mostly the blind
from the state school down the street.
They gaze at the tv's flawed picture: wrestlers
limned in blue light, the feminine soothing
of the trainer's hands. Beside me
at her table, Nina strokes her dog
to calmness, tilts her third bourbon.
Once, she told me how her mother
had kept hidden for decades
the Lithuanian coins that blistered
her brother's eyes—dead at four of measles.
Across the scarred table her hands
flutter, moth wings, a touch soft
as my great-aunt's years ago
tracing my forehead, my lips.
She had cataracts, the eye's filming, milky
and named for falling water. In her sunporch
she read to me of rivers and palaces until I saw
the pages were all wrong, the words
mere remembered cadences. At dusk
when lamps came on they stood,
she said, haloed like angels.
She crossed her hands over my eyes
and closed me into the mind's

green pacific room. That night I prayed
for her, a child's bargaining with God.
Tonight, in a blue half-light
of faces, blindness seems immense
as the lucid hours of insomnia—
somewhere a scarf's shadow grows
dangerous over the clock's face
glowing with the numerals
of 3:16 a.m. In my hand
the glass is chilled and prayer
is simply waiting for the mind to float
into precision, to still. Soon
I'll drive home through flooded streets.
Nina in her room will change her wet dress
for a gown discovered slowly
by a system of tags and textures. I want her
then, to sit quietly, in a pure matrix
of imagined light, darkness pressing down
like rain as the radio plays stations
from Baton Rouge, New Orleans, and beyond.

Preparing the Estate Sale

This woman, this Marie Brousseau,
saved everything, a recluse receiving
foodstamp groceries, the medicines of old age.
I must soak her figurines in water
that darkens as dust floats from their skirts.
Air will dry them, high summer and magnolias choking
the house. Crystal wine stems glitter
on shelves among dolls turned
so their porcelain faces view the walls,
washed now where Marie scrawled private arguments
in China marker—opening in English, ending
in the imperfect time of French verbs.
But this damp. This kitchen. This plaster.

How do I assess the last twenty years:
the way she tested her eyesight daily with charts,
the large E faltering over the stove, the vanity
and this accretion of dresses?
Generations of her hats litter
the divan behind me, afternoon diminishing
as I mark buttonhooks and beaded purses in this shocked air
there's nothing delicate about, these paper sacks
on shelves in every room—vials of tannic acid,
charcoal and milk of magnesium, her Universal Poison Antidote.

Polishing the legs of chairs, the only toxin
is time—my face in the mirror,
clocks throughout the house arranged
by a private chronology, as if she could reverse
the way our lives pass so gracelessly from our hands.

She's younger in these photos than I am:
1925, Marie disembarks from France, New Orleans,
her face under a cloche, eyes vague smudges.
The dock must have smelled of oysters and chicory.
Or here, she reclines in a wicker chaise,
one of those green and cream evenings
the South is famous for, deep June.
She looks frankly at the camera, as if the future
would be kind, as if her life
could never drift unmoored.

Marie, I'm talking to you now. I'm asking you
who will smooth the wrinkles from my dresses?
Will it be someone so unknown
as to be past imagining? Someone discarding
my husband's letters, these notes to myself falling
contagious as leaves in this green hushed light
that indicts everything.
May they not judge us severely.

THREE

Chinese New Year

The dragon is in the street dancing beneath windows
    pasted with colored squares, past the man
who leans into the phone booth's red pagoda, past
    crates of doves and roosters veiled

until dawn. Fireworks complicate the streets
    with sulphur as people exchange gold
and silver foil, money to appease ghosts
    who linger, needy even in death. I am

almost invisible. Hands could pass through me
    effortlessly. This is how it is
to be so alien that my name falls from me, grows
    untranslatable as the shop signs,

the odors of ginseng and black fungus that idle
    in the stairwell, the corridor where
the doors are blue mouths ajar. Hands
    gesture in the smoke, the partial moon

of a face. For hours the soft numeric
    click of mah-jongg tiles drifts
down the hallway where languid Mai trails
    her musk of sex and narcotics.

There is no grief in this, only the old year
    consuming itself, the door knob blazing
in my hand beneath the light bulb's electric jewel.
    Between voices and fireworks

wind works bricks to dust—*hush, hush*—
    no language I want to learn. I can touch

the sill worn by hands I'll never know
   in this room with its low table

where I brew chrysanthemum tea. The sign
   for Jade Palace sheds green corollas
on the floor. It's dangerous to stand here
   in the chastening glow, darkening

my eyes in the mirror with the gulf of the rest
   of my life widening away from me, waiting
for the man I married to pass beneath
   the sign of the building, to climb

the five flights and say his Chinese name for me.
   He'll rise up out of the puzzling streets
where men pass bottles of rice liquor, where
   the new year is liquor, the black bottle

the whole district is waiting for, like
   some benevolent arrest—the moment
when men and women turn to each other and dissolve
   each bad bet, every sly mischance,

the dalliance of hands. They turn in lamplight
   the way I turn now. Wai Min is in the doorway.
He brings fish. He brings lotus root.
   He brings me ghost money.

Arias, 1971

It was her hair I always noticed, rippling
as she walked the hallway to our flat
below the opera singer who'd rehearse
until evening, her arias. China Doll battled
sometimes with her AWOL junkie lover—curses

and plates shattering the wall. Her son
sputtered airplane sounds and beat the radiator
with a spoon, wise already to what smoulders
out of helplessness. I closed my door.
When autumn turned bitter, we taped newspaper

over the panes and those winter nights
we rode the subway from Symphony to Chinatown
where I poured drinks at the Phoenix
and she hustled bars, the gambling houses.
The train rocked and windows gave our faces back

ghost twins, sisters from some other life.
China brushed her hair, coal black, until
it sparked, and if I closed my eyes the rails sang
raven wing, forbidden heart, bright cinder.
One long dusk I sat as her child

practiced his numbers, 5's and the 8's
he'd scrawl like those botched infinities
I'd drawn in high school notebooks
below the signs for man and woman, the sign
for death. China leaned over her spoon,

the match's wavering blue tongue,
over the shadow and soft skin of her arm.

Nothing to lose, she laughed,
nothing. Her strap slid from her shoulder
to show the crescent scar above her breast.

She slow danced with herself across the room,
vagrant hair swaying. Swaying, her face tilted
heavenward and the low pulse in her throat.
Upstairs the opera singer began again
Desdemona's final prayers for mercy

from a silent God. The aria soared and fell
and carried us out to December streets
milling with late shoppers, their breath chilled,
perishable, the season a paradise of dolls
and trains, the steaming subway vents.

That last time I saw her, we walked the blocks
to Washington, paused at a shopwindow: a pyramid
of televisions all tuned to Walter Cronkite.
His mouth shaped silent phrases. And then it began—
the roll call of war dead. Their names sailing

upward, ash, and we had everything
to lose. Snowing, and the wind lashed
China's hair, a hand
across her face, mine.
I tell you, it was snowing.

Hollywood Jazz

Who says it's cool says wrong.
   For it rises from the city's
      sweltering geometry of rooms,

fire escapes, and flares from the heels
   of corner boys on Occidental
      posing with small-time criminal

intent—all pneumatic grace. This
   is the music that plays at the moment
      in every late-night *noir* flick

when the woman finds herself alone, perfectly
   alone, in a hotel room before a man
      whose face is so shadowed as to be

invisible, one more bedroom arsonist
   seeing nothing remotely
      cool: a woman in a cage

of half-light, Venetian blinds.
   This is where jazz blooms, in the hook
      and snag of her zipper opening to

an enfilade of trumpets. Her dress
   falls in a dizzy indigo riff.
      I know her vices are minor: sex,

forgetfulness, the desire to be someone,
   anyone else. On the landing, the man
      pauses before descending

one more flight. Checks his belt. Adjusts
        the snap brim over his face. She smoothes
            her platinum hair and smokes a Lucky

to kill his cologne. And standing there
        by the window in her slip, midnight blue,
            the stockings she did not take off,

she is candescent, her desolation
        a music so voluptuous I want
            to linger with her. And if I do not

turn away from modesty or shame,
        I'm in this for keeps, flying with her
            into fear's random pivot where each article

glistens like evidence: the tube of lipstick,
        her discarded earrings. When she closes
            her eyes, she hears the streetcar's

nocturne up Jackson, a humpbacked sedan
        rounding the corner from now
            to that lavish void of tomorrow,

a sequence of rooms: steam heat, modern,
        2 bucks. Now listen. Marimbas.
            His cologne persists, a redolence

of fire alarms, and Darling,
        there are no innocents here, only
            dupes, voyeurs. On the stairs

he flicks dust from his alligator
        shoes. I stoop to straighten
            the seams of my stockings, and

when I meet him in the shadows
of the stairwell, clarinets whisper
Here, take my arm. Walk with me.

The Charmed Hour

—*for my mother*

On the radio, gypsy jazz. Django Reinhardt
   puts a slow fire to Ellington's *Solitude*
      while ice cubes pop in your martini. The sting
of lime on my palm. By the sink you lean,
   twisting your rings. Turn to the window.

In shadow you could be sixteen
   again, in your mother's kitchen
      above Cleveland, the cafés of Warsaw still
smoky in your mind with talk and cigarettes,
   English still a raw mystery of verbs.

Windows brighten across the city at the hour
   when voices steam from the street
      like some sadness—the charmed hour
when, smooth as brilliantine, Phil Verona
   with his Magic Violin slides from the radio.

Ice-blue in silk, his All-Girl Orchestra sways
   through the parlor. You let yourself
      step with them, let a gardenia release
its vanilla scent in your hair.
   Over terraces, you dance above vapor-lights,

Gold Coast streets where club doors swing
   like the doors of banks that never fail.
      In back rooms men and women spend themselves
over green baize tables, the ivory poker chips.
   In their chests wings beat, steady

as the longing wakened to from every dream
    of flying. We could shut the door
        on this vertigo, but Mother when we
come to ourselves our feet skim the tiles.
    Spoons shine on the table, and Mother,

we're dancing. I'm mouthing the words
    to a song I never knew, singing when
        evening arrives and flattens the sky
to a last yellow crease of light,
    thin as a knife, as a wish.

The Floating Wedding

Awake she's wedded to the stranger
in herself, her hands in climateless light,

nails smooth and blue. Nothing has changed.
Her husband sleeps. The cabin fills

with slight bitterness, carnations
returning their small fires to air.

Nothing has changed. The wedding over,
guests ferried back to the pier, only

artifacts of marriage remain, heavy knives,
the wedding cake sodden and littered

with the confetti of good cheer.
She watches on shore a single headlamp.

It's the drunk. She knows him, has seen him
in the streets of the village, knows

he's been asked to leave the homosexual bars,
the slim forbidden boys with faces dark

and watery as those in aquatints. Nightly
he struggles with the bicycle through sand

past floating piers and houses with their freight
of sleep. She'd like to spare the old man

his blind driving into night
a little while. She'd like to sit and drink,

maybe talk or ease his trembling,
incurable as the singleness returned to

after passion. Turning away
she lowers her veil to the sea,

its crown of flowers floating
like a doll's small funeral barge.

When she wraps her arms around herself
she is wrapped in a blue fire. She touches

her husband's whitening shoulder. She'll sleep
and not witness the way the old man

suffers dawn, not witness
the night moving off over the sea,

drifting with its burden of longing
to darken the other half of the world.

Remington

It's hot—the evening could so easily erupt
to a fusillade of sirens. Then I'd take the arm
of a passing stranger, whirl him startled
in a brisk flamenco. There'd be a knife,
some roses. But these are the vapors of summer.

I sit on the railing, smoke, and watch
the teenage mothers of Remington stroll
their babies, shaking back their razor-cut hair
to the wail of blues rolling through the screens
of narrow apartments. Evenly, the words wash

the faces of men on stoops in stained workshirts,
half-moons of grease under their nails, the faces
of the unemployed who have all day taken refuge
from the blinding streets in the museums
of pool halls and taverns, over the women

fanning themselves, crescents of sweat spoiling
their sleeveless dresses. There's nothing to do
about it, but see the shapes the music makes
of us, as if we were moved by some larger volition:
across the street, A-Jay's out of jail delivered

by the seamless hands of the Public Defender.
The neighbor woman told me how, wild one night
last week, he shot out each mirror in the house,
then stayed locked inside for hours. She waved
the air between us, clucked softly to herself.

Quiet tonight, he sits in the doorway,
loose change in his pockets and the Pimlico sheet

inked with the numbers and handicaps of each stable.
Each horse scrawled on a paper scrap, arranged,
rearranged. Around a cigarette, he mutters

the sweet inflammatory names: Mere Scintilla,
Lark's Dream, Fair Charleen, and everything
they spell of the miraculous legs that bear
such violent hopes. Chestnuts and bays
sport jockey's bright silks, glories fleeting

as the current of wind that lifts and eddies
his paper scraps. Lately,
these details are precious to me:
a cigarette's fiery arc, the brief filigree
of shadow across a stranger's shoulders

as night falls and catches the voice
of Jay's woman. Framed in the doorway,
she bends, gathers the scattered notations.
She tells her friend, *When he gets this way,
he just tears my clothes off. Just tears them off.*

Housekeeping Cottages

A tin flamingo rhumbas with a mermaid,
their thin music spins through the window
to Harry tipped back in his deck chair,
his cigarette making smoke patches over
the Monopoly board. When he squints, the smoke blends
with the breaker's foam. His kids scream
at the tideline, their beach ball bobbing
in surf, mild and green.

Dot brings back two cold ones he opens
with a church key. Each summer they leave
Jersey's industrial stacks,
the sun blazing off the sides
of aluminum diners. Harry likes the rows
of saltboxes shuttered clean
in blue, the long terra-cotta walkway that banks
and curves into the seawall. He likes the riffle
of play money, the way the game lasts
all vacation. It's Dot's turn

and she shakes the dice a long time.
He likes the sound and the sense of his life
edging the sea. She throws and Harry watches
her thigh tense, her legs big,
absolutely smooth. When she leans to read
the dice, Jungle Gardenia wafts across
the table. Her flatiron scrapes to Marvin Gardens
and the kids are screaming, running
after the shadow of a blimp, their mouths
small black circles.

In his palm the racecar token warms
as he waits for Dot to oil her shoulders.
He doesn't mind waiting. He can do it for hours
like sometimes at night smoking
hearing the sea's invisible drag. That's when
he thinks about the Olds, robin's-egg blue,
he longs for. The wheels would shine
and ride him smoothly down the avenues,
a little dangerous, passing hotels and women
in doorways with permed blonde haloes.

He drops his cigarette into an empty.
It sizzles as he lights another, then rolls.
A double, two sixes. He roars his car
down Boardwalk, its diamonds and expensive faces.
Past GO, hit the bank and cruise the purple
side streets, Mediterranean and Baltic. At Chance
Harry draws a card. Harry goes to jail
and does not collect. In the sky
the blimp looks like a slim cigar
its wrapper unfurling behind it, a banner
Harry can't make out.

Spring

If only we'd arrived without history
at this room thick with columns
of steam. No stairways leading
up or down, only this room given to sky,

eclipsing the garden, the bottling plant,
and mill houses. Then all I'd need
to know would be here among towels,
the porcelain tub and shock of forsythia

slipping my fingers down each vertebra
of the spine's perishable harp. These shy
wings—your shoulders which have stooped
all day over sorrowing accounts.

Light pierces the pane, glazes water
spilling from my hands over your hair.
This thin vein across your temple.
The factory whistle shrills and men walk

from locked trunks to their cars
at that time once called *the gloaming*
when the sky holds a dense glow
and voices shimmer then drift like shadows

netted among the branches of mulberry
and linden below the porch where we linger
over shrimp, Greek cheese. It's April,
the evening's cool and far off

the neon advertisements speak
only to themselves. They remind you

of the tangled circuits of your father's mind,
injured months ago—a drunken accident

on winter roads. Sometimes he mistakes you
for his brother or a younger self,
his workman's hands dangling, tapered
long like yours, but awkward

in the hospital gown's loose folds.
Because sleep is difficult he watches
all night the hills of the city hammered
with light, the halfmoon blazing

steep streets, mazes of alleys
and cul de sacs that carried us to this turning,
calmly entering each other's histories.
Difficult son of that father, I'll hold you

until we arrive at a radical simplicity:
this room suspended over trees enlarging
in the deep vault of spring,
your damp hair cool against my cheek.

Invisible Gestures

The way geodes can be cracked to reveal ears
perfectly listening to crystal, you could crack
open this picture and find anything.
A man, a woman in scarves
at a table
that like the sea and sky behind them
might, at any moment,
vaporize into blue. Netted
with invisible gestures
sky and sea persist
the only certainty in our traveling.

For it's possible she has been traveling
all night. A train
with frame after frame
unraveling behind her. Pastures where cows continue
in the dark, unseen. Station lights
pin faces into the ivory of untroubled repose,
the repose of long waiting
for a scheduled event. Perhaps
she is traveling to leave her face behind,
an unremarkable woman closer to *thirty-five*
than herself. She notices telephone wires
link the country with the urgency
and tenuousness of a late-night call.

It is possible the man has been sleepless,
waiting. Maybe failing to reconstruct
the floor plans of every place
he has ever lived, he strikes a match.
In the flame his palm curls toward him,

shell-pink as a waiting ear,
and for the first time, down streets,
he hears the chain of desire and expectation
that moves the world. His cigarette smoke
will stop at the ceiling
as in the frame of this moment
every street, every track narrows
into a point of blue.

As the shadows and halftones of their nights
contain the day's salvation,
it's possible they believe,
even at this late date,
beyond the surface
a man and a woman shelter a miracle,
the salt of their hands.

Accretion

Consider autumn,
   its violent candling
      of hours: birches

& beach plums flare harsh,
   chrome-yellow, orange,
      the dog zigzags the hillside

tangled with flaming vines
   to the pond below & barks
      at the crows' reflected flight,

a reverse swimming
   among water lilies, that
      most ancient of flowers

anchored by muscular stems
   in the silt of cries
      & roots, tenacious as the mind's

common bloom, remembered men
   I have touched at night
      in the room

below the African painter's
   empty loft, his few abandoned
      canvases, narratives

of drought & famine, of how
   his people, hands linked
      entered the deepest cave,

the unbearable heart
of belief where each gesture
encloses the next—clouds

packed densely as ferns, becoming
coal, the final diamond
of light, the god's return

as rain, its soft insistence
loosening the yellowed hands
of leaves that settle

at my feet. How expendable
& necessary this mist
in my hair, these jewels

beading the dog's wet coat.
How small I am
beneath this vast sway.

THE
JUNIPER
PRIZE

This volume is the twelfth recipient
of the Juniper Prize
presented annually by the
University of Massachusetts Press
for a volume of original poetry.
The prize is named in honor of Robert Francis,
who has lived for many years at
Fort Juniper, Amherst, Massachusetts.